The MOTHER'S PICTURE ALPHABET

Illustrated by
HENRY ANELAY

With a new Introduction by
PETER STOCKHAM

Dover Publications, Inc., New York

Published in Canada by General Publishing Company, Ltd.,
30 Lesmill Road, Don Mills, Toronto, Ontario.
Published in the United Kingdom by Constable and
Company, Ltd., 10 Orange Street, London WC 2.

This Dover edition, first published in 1974, is an unabridged
republication of the work originally published by S. W. Partridge
at the Office of the Children's Friend, No. 9 Paternoster Row,
London, in 1862. Peter Stockham has written a new Introduction
especially for this Dover edition.

International Standard Book Number: 0-486-23089-9
Library of Congress Catalog Card Number: 74-75846

Manufactured in the United States of America
Dover Publications, Inc.
180 Varick Street
New York, N.Y. 10014

Introduction to the Dover Edition

Published in 1862, *The Mother's Picture Alphabet* was immediately acclaimed by the critics: "The handsomest book of its kind offered to the general public . . ." *(Athenaeum);* "As regards illustration, type, paper, and binding, NOTHING illustrative of the *Alphabet* has, we imagine, been yet produced, which will bear the REMOTEST comparison with it. . . ." *(Illustrated London News).* Its permitted dedication to the Princess Beatrice, and its mention under the letter *Q* of

> Our own dear Victoria, who rules o'er the land;
> For whom we all pray, with one heart and one tongue,
> That her reign may be happy, and useful, and long . . .

sets the *Alphabet* in the historic years of Victoria's reign, with its accepted values both religious and domestic. The *Alphabet* presents a rural ideal ("Milkmaid, who sits there, with round rosy cheek"), which the majority of its readers would still know from experience, and a picture of domestic security and routine which children have always loved. Its range, both in things mentioned and objects illustrated, is surprisingly wide; and it is claimed that over 300 of the items mentioned in the letterpress are to be found in the pictures. To us the interest is often in seeing objects no longer used set within the pictures or on the page: the Bandbox, the Gig, the Organ Grinder, the Image-Boy, the Slate. A radical social conscience can be seen at times, for example in its concern for slavery, and under *U* it is interesting to see:

> Union—how strong, in the picture we see,
> Where five men, united, pull down that great tree . . .

Part of the explanation for these social views can be found in the nature of the publisher. The title page tells us that the book is published "at the office of the Children's Friend," and the dedication to Princess Beatrice is curiously signed by "The Editor of the 'British Workman.' " The publisher was S. W. Partridge, and his initials appear at the end of the poem on the last leaf. He published the works of Clara Lucas Balfour including that most famous of juvenile temperance works originally called *The Juvenile Abstainer* and later retitled *Morning Dew Drops* (also illustrated by Henry Anelay), and the attractive *A Mother's Lessons on the Lord's Prayer.* The *British Work-*

man was a penny magazine started in 1855 "with the earnest desire of promoting the health, wealth, and happiness of the industrial classes." From its commencement it used well-known illustrators such as George Cruikshank, John Gilbert, Harrison Weir, and Henry Anelay, who was one of the most frequent contributors. *The British Workman* was still going strong in 1892 when an advertisement by S. W. Partridge showed him also publishing such other monthly magazines as *The Children's Friend, The Infant's Magazine, The Family Friend,* and *The Mother's Companion,* which were bound into volumes for sale as Annuals.

Almost nothing is known about Henry Anelay as a person, but he was a prolific book and magazine illustrator. In addition to his work on the *Alphabet* and other books for Partridge he drew the illustrations which Beeton Dickes color-printed for one of the earliest *Robinson Crusoe's* to appear in color in England (also in 1862). The *Alphabet* was produced in three different editions: in boards at five shillings (about 50 cents); in cloth, lettered with red edges, at seven shillings and sixpence; and in cloth, elegant, at ten shillings and sixpence, a high price for a child's book in those days, and obviously designed for display in the drawing room.

The values and the moral messages are thus carefully presented to satisfy an increasingly educated artisan class and a middle-class audience. The household reflected in the text and illustrations is not that of the rich, but it is very comfortable. It has at least one servant and a nurse, and law and order prevail. The postman calls "at hovels and halls," and the policeman "who goes round to see all is safe at night" carries his bull's-eye lantern with him. The order of things is set, and moral precepts rule accepted behavior. The message is repeated:

> Envy, vexation at others' success:
> How well it would be if we thought of self less!
>
> Gentle and Good—can we say this of you?
>
> Lie, that no good child would ever dare tell.

Although less pronounced these days, much of the warmth given out by this book is of the kind to appeal to us even today:

> Quilt, the warm cover, so carefully spread,
> By nurse's kind hands, on my snug little bed.

As a classic of Victorian book illustration it still has its appeal to children as well as much to interest their parents.

PETER STOCKHAM

London, April 1974

THE MOTHER'S
PICTURE ALPHABET.

FEED MY LAMBS

S. JOHN. XXI. XV.

THE MOTHER'S PICTURE ALPHABET

DESIGNED BY
HENRY ANELAY.

DEDICATED BY HER MAJESTY'S PERMISSION
TO H.R.H. THE
PRINCESS BEATRICE

ENGRAVED BY
JAMES JOHNSTON

PUBLISHED AT THE OFFICE OF THE CHILDREN'S FRIEND
N.º 9 PATERNOSTER ROW:
LONDON.

LONDON:
PRINTED BY G. WATSON,
Kirby St., Hatton Garden.

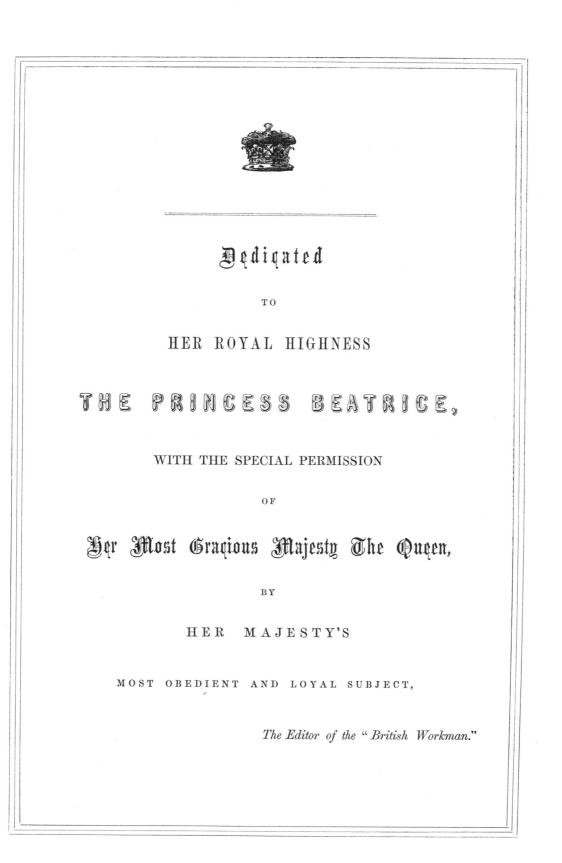

Dedicated

TO

HER ROYAL HIGHNESS

THE PRINCESS BEATRICE,

WITH THE SPECIAL PERMISSION

OF

Her Most Gracious Majesty The Queen,

BY

HER MAJESTY'S

MOST OBEDIENT AND LOYAL SUBJECT,

The Editor of the " British Workman."

CHILDREN should be encouraged to find out *for themselves* the various objects that are introduced into the illustrations. It has not been practicable to engrave *all* the objects that are named in the letterpress, but upwards of 300 of them are to be found in the pictures, thus affording ample scope for exercising the ingenuity and perseverance of the little ones.

TRAIN UP A
CHILD IN THE WAY HE
SHOULD GO: AND WHEN HE
IS OLD, HE WILL NOT
DEPART FROM IT.

Proverbs xxii. 6.

A —my dear child—the first letter—is here:

One that in many a word does appear.

A begins **A**rch, under which, in the rain,

We sheltered awhile till the sun shone again.

A begins **A**pple, so juicy and sweet,

That, when ripe in **A**utumn, we all like to eat.

A begins **A**corn,—the oak's seed, you know:

How strange that from it such a great tree should grow!

Anchor, made strong, the deep sea-bed to grip;

That stops in a moment the mightiest ship.

A begins **A**ngel, that dwells far above.

Also dear **A**unt, whom we all of us love.

Young cousins, **A**da, and **A**lice, and **A**nn:

Albert;—and **A**rthur, who'll soon be a man.

Pious king **A**lfred,—a good King indeed!

Abel, of whom in the Bible we read:

Abraham, **A**aron, and many a name,

That stands in that record for praise or for blame.

But, till you are able to search for them there,

Ask dearest mamma to explain who they were.

B begins Bible, the book we so prize;

That teaches us all to be holy and wise.

B begins Boy, in a studious mood,

While others blow Bubbles, or stray in the wood.

Also Balloon, that soars up in the sky:

I should not much like to be mounting so high.

Bramble, on which, when the autumn comes round,

The Blackberry cluster is sure to be found.

B begins Butterfly, coloured so gay;

Also the Bee, out at work all the day.

B begins Boat, lying there in the sun;

Also the Beach, a nice spot for a run.

Bellows, that helps us to kindle the fire.

Brush, that to keep our hair smooth we require.

Bell, that bright, pretty and tinkling thing,

That, when little Susan is wanted, we ring.

Bandbox—we all know what that is, no doubt;

And Basket—a thing we could scarce do without.

Bag, that dear Robert to school with him takes;

And Broom, for the litter the fading rose makes.

C begins Child, with her
fine hat and band;

Carlo, her dog, that she pats with
her hand.

Chair, where he sits, with its Cushion so soft.

C begins Cowslip, that grows in the Croft.

Also Carnation—how sweet its perfume!—

And Crocus, that in the cold spring loves to bloom.

Church, where we all love on Sunday to go.

Castle, that towers o'er the country below.

Cherry, a nice fruit, so shining and sweet.

Corn, that, when ground, forms the bread that we eat.

Coal,—for the winter an excellent thing.

Cuckoo, a strange bird that sings in the spring.

Cock, that each morning awakes us from sleep.

Cascade, where the waters rush down with a leap.

Cat, our own pussy, that so loves to play,

And all mamma's Cotton unrolled yesterday.

Cow, that afar in the meadow we see,

And gives us nice milk for our breakfast and tea.

Christmas, a season that soon will be here,

And join friends again that are pleasant and dear.

D begins Doll, that the children, you see,

Have dressed up as fine as a doll need to be.

D begins Dove, too,—a fond, gentle bird,

Of whose loving nature we often have heard.

Damson, a fruit very nice in a pie;

And Deer—in the park there how graceful they lie!

The Dahlia, one of our handsomest flowers;

And Daisy, that dear little favourite of ours.

D begins Dog, but I hope he won't tease

Those pretty young Ducks sailing under the trees.

Drover, who, with his stick under his arm,

Drives back, every evening, the herd to the farm.

D begins Door, where Jane hangs up her shawl.

Darkness—when night overshadows us all.

Dunce, a bad child who refuses to learn.

Dinner, so nice when from walk we return.

Dumpling and Duchess, Day, Dreamer, and Dirt.

Daniel, who stayed with the lions unhurt.

David, who grew, from a boy at the fold,

A great king, and wrote us those fine Psalms of old.

E begins Egg, in the
bird's pretty nest:
May no rude hand its dear treasures
molest.

Also a large one, just boiled in a cup:

I dare say our Edward would soon eat it up.

Ewe, how she fondles the lamb at her side!

Eagle, that soars to the clouds in his pride.

Elder, with ripe purple berries bedecked.

Earthquake—see how the poor houses are wrecked.

Easel, where, sketching, the young artist sat:

I wish I could draw such an Engine as that.

Elm, a tall tree, that spreads out in the sky.

Earth, that we live on: Example, and Eye.

Elk, a wild animal, horned like a stag.

Empire, a kingdom; and Ensign, a flag.

East, where, each morning, we see the sun rise.

Elephant, too, of so monstrous a size.

Ellen, our cousin, so dear to us all:

Some Evening perhaps we will give her a call.

Envy, vexation at others' success:

How well it would be if we thought of self less!

F begins Fanny, whose dear brother, Fred,

Has got a large basket of Fruit on his head.

How pleased she appears, with her armful of Flowers.

So Fragrant and Fresh, after yesterday's showers.

F begins Football—what capital Fun!—

Again it flies up, and how fast the lads run!

Ford, where in shallowest water they wade.

Fern, like green Feathers, adorning the glade.

Fir, a dark tree that towers up in the sky.

Fox, a strange animal, cunning and sly.

Fawn, a young deer, very gentle and meek.

Friday, the last day but one in the week.

Feather, like what baby wears in his hat:

The dear little fellow—so Fair and so Fat.

France, a fine country, and nearest our own:

May we be rivals in goodness alone.

Fender, a guard that protects from the Fire.

Food,—the good things that our bodies require.

Famine—a dearth, a great scarceness of bread:

Oh let us be thankful if we are well fed.

G begins Grandpa: how baby does stare

At the pretty Gold watch he is showing him there!

Greyhound, a dog very nimble and slim ;

The fastest of runners would never catch him.

Goat, that can clamber up hills steep and high.

Gooseberries—Grandma shall make you a pie.

Grasshopper, too, that sings loud in the Grass.

Grapes, uncle grows in his Greenhouse of Glass.

Gig—how the horse there does gallop along !

Also Guitar, very sweet with a song.

Gleaner, the Girl there, who stands at the Gate.

Guard, that surrounds the large nursery Grate.

GOD, the great Maker and Father of all.

Globe, like a map on a very large ball.

Gardener—see he is hoeing the Ground,

Or else in the Garden rank weeds would abound.

Gnat, that at eve dances under the tree.

Goose, that so white on the common we see.

Gold, a bright metal of yellowish hue.

Gentle and Good—can we say this of you ?

H begins Hen—fond affec-
tionate thing !—

Observe how she hides her brood

under her wing:

Hovel, where nightly they shelter and sleep.

Hive, the bees' Home, where their Honey they keep.

H begins Henry, with Hand on his Hoop:

Young Herbert's Hat, too, who by him does stoop.

Hay, that the Haymakers pile in a cart.

Humble—a lowly and teachable Heart.

Hook, often used to hang anything on.

Horse—when I'm bigger, I'll ride behind John.

Horn—on the river it sounds very sweet.

Hamper, a basket for things nice to eat.

Hoe, by whose Help we root weeds up with ease.

Hatchet, so useful in cutting down trees.

Hyacinths wild, that in shady woods grow;

Hollyhocks, too, what a beautiful show!

Harrow, for breaking the clods—a spiked frame.

Helen, my favourite playfellow's name.

House—why 'tis dear grandpapa's, I declare;

He's opened the Hothouse, to give his plants air.

I begins Infant, with fat cheeks and hands:
How upright, beside Isabella, she stands!

Ibex, a creature with horns like a goat.

Inkstand—John writes such a beautiful note!

Ivy, that covers, as though with a screen,

Papa's garden-wall with its leafage so green.

Island, a place circled round by the sea.

Image-boy—few look so cheerful as he.

Ibis, a bird, that in Egypt, I've read,

Was worshipped while living, and honoured when dead.

Ice—very wintry and dark is the sky,

But the skaters across it seem almost to fly.

Ice-berg, so tall, in the cold Arctic seas.

Icicles—see how they hang from the trees!

India, a country far distant from ours.

Iris, too, one of our gay garden flowers.

Invalid, out in his wheel-chair, when fine:—

How thankful I should be if health is but mine!

Ivory, hard—the great elephant's teeth.

Idler   he'll never wear honour's bright wreath.

J j

begins Judge: he looks rather severe,

But they who act rightly have nothing to fear.

Jaguar, a tiger, that haunts wooded rocks.

Jackal, an animal much like a fox.

Jet,—how it sparkles against the tall trees!

Junk, a strange vessel, used by the Chinese.

Jug, that, each morning, Jane fills at the spring.

Justice—in all men an excellent thing.

Jewel, a precious and glittering stone.

Jam—very nice, as most children will own.

Jay, the harsh singer, most country lads know.

Jars—in the pantry they stand in a row.

Jonquil, a flower that in spring loves to bloom.

Jasmine, that breathes all around its perfume.

June and July—summer months in our year.

Juggler; and Jetty, a small wooden pier.

Jacob, and Jonah, and Jesse, and James—

You'll learn, by-and-bye, about these Bible names.

And, greater than all, by each Christian adored,

JESUS, the name of our Saviour and Lord.

begins **Kite**, that we saw in the sky: It vanished almost, it was soaring so high.

Kittens, that frisk by their old mother's side,

Who watches their gambols with fondness and pride.

Kangaroo: **K**it, too, a vessel of wood.

Kitchen, where Ann cooks our dinner, so good.

Kettle, at tea-time that sings on the fire.

Keys, that to open our locks we require.

Kiln, where the labourers are burning the lime:

I've strolled down among them there, many a time.

Kite, that so swift pounces down on its prey.

Kingfisher, too, with its plumage so gay.

Knit, as mamma does, when evening comes on.

Knife, such as dear uncle brought us for John.

Knee—without this we could scarce walk about.

Kindness—we all know what that is, no doubt.

Kate, our dear auntie, who asked us to tea:

She gave such a **K**iss to my brother and me.

King, a great monarch, so mighty and grand.

Kent, a fine county, the pride of our land.

L begins Lighthouse, that

shows a great **Light**,

To guide the poor sailor at sea in the

night.

Lightning, that darts from the black angry sky.

Ladder, that helps us to reach very high.

Lemon, a yellow fruit, juicy and sour.

Lily, a lovely and sweet-scented flower.

Lupins, so blue, in the garden that grow.

Larkspur: and Lilac,—a beautiful show.

Leopard: and Lion, well known for his roar.

Loaf, that the baker's man brings to the door.

Lane, where in summer the roses we find.

Lamp, that we use when for reading inclined.

Lavender, prized for its perfume so sweet.

Lantern, that lights, in the darkness, our feet.

Lie, that no good child would ever dare tell.

Lock, that secures our great street-door so well.

Leaves, that in autumn the garden bestrew.

Love, the fond feeling I have, dear, for you.

Letter: and Ladle, a large iron spoon.

Lamb: also Lime tree, that blossoms in June.

M begins Moor, where, so barren and still,

The path winds along close beside the old **Mill**.

Mountain, that towers up aloft in the sky:

'Twould take us a long time to clamber so high.

Mist, that, in autumn, rolls up the hill-side.

Mouse, that so loves in the pantry to hide.

Melon, a large fruit, with rough, barky rind.

Mushroom, that oft in the Morning we find.

Moon, that, at evening, so calm and so bright,

On all things around sheds her pale silver light.

Music—we all like to play and to sing.

May-bloom, that covers the hedge in the spring.

Mower, who stands in the Meadow, so blythe,

And cuts down the grass with his well-sharpen'd scythe.

Milkmaid, who sits there, with round rosy cheek:

The cow standing by her, so patient and meek.

Monkey—a mischievous creature is he.

Milk-can, that holds the nice Milk for our tea.

Macaw, much admired for his gay-coloured wings:

And Magpie, who loves to hoard glittering things.

N begins News-boy, with

papers to sell:

What a good thing it must be to

learn to read well!

At **N**ine, he leaves one at each customer's door;

And by **N**oon he will sell all he carries, and more.

Nuts, such as Willie, our **N**ephew so good,

Brought in a bag from the neighbouring wood.

Nest, that we spied in the coppice to-day:

(We never take one of the birds' eggs away).

Nettle, a weed that is found everywhere;

And badly it stings, if you do not take care.

Nurse, who so gently soothes baby to sleep.

Night, when the stars from the firmament peep.

Needy, like Jones's poor children, so sad:

I gave them to-day all the halfpence I had.

Newcastle, famed for the coal that we use;

Also **N**orthampton, for strong boots and shoes.

Noah, whom God in the great ark shut in,

Before He would drown the bad world for its sin.

Good **N**ehemiah, whose heart was so pained,

To see how his country the Sabbath profaned.

begins **Organ**: the tune
is so gay,

The children could stand there and

listen all day.

Here, give the lad this, and let dear baby see;

How he stares at the figures in wonder and glee!

O begins Orange, a fruit you well know.

Oak, the strong tree on which acorns do grow.

Ostrich, a bird whose fine feathers we prize.

Onions, that Jane of the greengrocer buys.

Owl, a strange bird, that at night loves to hoot.

Opossum, an animal; Olive, a fruit.

Omnibus—how I should like a long ride,

If dear Uncle George could but sit by my side!

Oyster, whose shells are collected by boys,

And made into grottoes with shouting and noise.

Order,—arrangement; by method and rule.

Oscar, the boy that we met with at school.

Oats, that the Ostler gives Jack every day.

Otter, that loves in the water to play.

Obelisk, too, a tall pillar of stone,

Inscribed with the deeds that our great men have done.

P begins **Prayer**, such as dear little Ned

Beside Mamma prayed before going to bed.

P begins Primrose, a pretty spring flower.

Parasol, useful in sunshine and shower.

Plum, a nice fruit, very good in a pie.

Pear, such as often at market we buy.

Plough, that in spring o'er the rough field is drawn.

Peacock, a fine bird that struts on the lawn.

Poplar, a tree very slender and tall.

Pie; and Plum-pudding, that pleases us all.

Pen, that we write with; and Postman, who calls,

With letters and packets, at hovels and halls.

Also Policeman, with bull's-eye so bright,

Who goes round to see all is safe in the night.

Pail, that Jane carries about when she cleans.

Palm-tree, so common in all Eastern scenes.

Padlock, with which Papa fastens the gate.

Pole, a long tree-stem, so tall and so straight.

Pelican, Parrot—birds very well known.

Pickaxe: and Pillar, a column of stone.

Q begins Queen, in her jewels, so grand—
Our own dear VICTORIA, who rules o'er the land;

For whom we all pray, with one heart and one tongue,

That her reign may be happy, and useful, and long.

Q begins Quarrel—one angry word,

And oh, what a host of bad passions are stirred!

Quill, that papa can make into a pen,

And with it write letters to dear brother Ben.

Quince, a nice fruit, like a large yellow pear,

That grows on a tree now become very rare.

Quagga, an animal; Quail, a plump bird,

Whose cry in the springtime we sometimes have heard.

Quarry, a pit where they dig out the stone,

Just down by the hill-side, so barren and lone.

Question, the word of inquiry we ask,

When difficult subjects occur in our task.

Quiet, the silence mamma bids us keep,

While trying to hush the dear baby to sleep.

Quilt, the warm cover, so carefully spread,

By nurse's kind hands, on my snug little bed.

R begins Rosa: how pleased she appears, To watch those plump **R**abbits, with long silky ears!

Rose, the fair flower with so sweet a perfume.

Rug, that in winter adorns our nice room.

Rainbow, that glows like an arch in the sky.

Rocks, that rise up in the ocean so high.

Rake, that is used to turn over the hay :

Rick, the tall pile when they store it away.

Robin, that hops to our door, in the snow.

Rook, whose strange cawing we all so well know.

River, where James goes to bathe every morn.

Reaper, the man who cuts down the ripe corn.

Rest, when we 're weary, most welcome and sweet.

Ribbon, that trims mamma's bonnet so neat.

Raspberries—see how they hang in the sun.

Rover, with Robert just out for a Run.

Rush, that the marshes and damp places fills.

Ravine, a deep hollow pass in the hills.

Ruth, the good maiden of whom you will read

Some day in God's book—a sweet story indeed.

S begins Slave. Who can
look, without pain,
On that agonised face, and that whip,
and that chain?

Squirrel, that acorns and nuts loves to hide.

String, with which Susan's great bandbox was tied.

Shell—on the beach what a number we found !

Spade, papa uses to dig up the ground.

Swan, that so gracefully floats on the stream.

Sun, that arises with silvery beam.

Strawberry, too, a soft fruit very sweet.

Shoes, papa buys me to wear on my feet.

Sleep, for dear baby ; and Shed, for the Sheep.

Sickle, a round knife, with which the men reap.

Spectacles, like grandma wears on her nose.

Snowdrop, the earliest spring flower that blows.

Ship, a large vessel that sails on the Sea.

Slate—mamma says she will buy one for me.

Sunday, the day when in God's house we bow.

Stool, like Jane sits on, when milking the cow.

Scissors, we cut with: Sieve, Sermon, and Shower.

And Sceptre, well known as the emblem of power.

T begins Tunnel, through

which went the **Train**

That brought Uncle **Thomas** and

me back again.

Ticket—the guard did not ask me for mine.

Telegraph, too, by the side of the line.

Trellis, the cross wood up which the plants grow.

Tulips, full blown, what a beautiful show!

Tea-party, given as Teacher's kind Treat;

With Table, Tray, Teapot, and Teacups so neat.

Trunk, the great Tree that the woodmen cut down

For Timber to build that great house in the Town.

Turnpike, a Toll-gate across the high road.

Throne, for the monarch: Tusk, Tiger, and Toad.

Thistle, a weed, very prickly and rank.

Thyme, the sweet plant that we found on the bank.

Trumpet, an instrument, loud, and so clear.

Torch, that, to light them at night, the men bear.

Traveller—see how he sits on the stile:

Perhaps he's been walking for many a mile.

Top—when you're older, I'll buy one for you.

Tongue—it should speak what is loving and true.

L

U begins Urn, that at tea-time Jane brings,

When we all love to hear how it hisses and sings.

Also Umbrella, that kept us so dry

When the heavy rain poured from the black angry sky.

Union—how strong, in the picture we see,

Where five men, united, pull down that great tree.

Union-jack, the famed flag of our land.

Usher, the second at school in command.

Unity, what we so love and approve—

Brothers with sisters, all dwelling in love.

Umpire, one picked from the wisest and best,

To settle disputes when two persons contest.

Untaught, like too many we see every day.

Uncommon, the singular, out-of-the-way.

Uzzah, who, heedless of what God had said,

And touching the ark with rash hands, was struck dead.

Underwood—bushes that grow among trees.

Uncle—a fine romp I had on his knees.

Up—a good word in our memory to keep,

When we wake in the morning, refresh'd, from our sleep.

V begins Van, such as,
last Whitsuntide,
Took out our school class for a holi-
day ride :

Viaduct, too, the arched road, high and strong,

On which our good horses went trotting along.

Village, the cluster of houses we passed:

And so we arrived at the common at last.

Vesture—sometimes made of Velvet—a dress.

Vanity, pride in the things we possess.

Vine, whose ripe grapes we all think such a treat.

Vessel, that holds our spring-water, so sweet.

Violin, Vincent is learning to play,

(He finds it not easy, I venture to say).

Volcano, a mountain that bursts into flame:

The picture contains one—Vesuvius, its name.

Violet, too, a most sweet-scented thing,

That often we meet with in woods, in the spring.

Vase, a large pot used for holding our flowers.

Verandah, that shelters from sunshine and showers.

Vagrant, who strays without home in the land.

Volume, a book, such as this in your hand.

W many a Word does begin;

As Water-wheel, Walnut, Wheat, Wheelbarrow, Win.

Wind, that blows over the common so strong:

It drives, as you see, the poor children along.

Ah, Walter, my boy, for your cap you must run;

Though William, behind, calls it capital fun.

Windmill, whose great sails but rarely stand still.

Waggon—the team has just come up the hill.

Well, that supplies us with Water to drink.

Willow, that droops by the cool river's brink.

Wasp, very fond of a plum or a peach.

Wreck—a sad sight, lying there on the beach.

Wallflower, that blossoms so fragrant in spring.

Wren—you should see him—the tiniest thing!

Wall, in our garden, where sweet roses climb.

Watch, like papa has, to tell him the time.

War, that disfigures our fair earth with blood.

Winter, that scatters the leaves in the Wood.

Wisdom, that Solomon asked of the Lord,

Above greatest things that the World could afford.

X

X

There are so few words

that begin with an **X**,

To find them would any poor writer

perplex;

And so, if you please, as the X for TEN stands,

We'll give you, in rhyme, God's ten solemn commands:—

I.
Worship the Lord God, thy Maker, alone;

II.
And bow not to idols of wood or of stone.

III.
Speak not God's name without reverence and awe,

Or He will reprove thee for breaking this law.

IV.
Remember the Sabbath, of all days the best:

Work six, keep the seventh for worship and rest.

V.
Honour thy parents, if thou wouldst live long.

VI.
Thou shalt not kill, with the sword or the tongue.

VII.
Avoid thoughts and actions unclean or impure.

VIII.
Beware that thou steal not, although thou be poor.

IX.
Thou no false witness 'gainst any shalt bear,

X.
Nor covet thy neighbour's more bountiful share.

Y begins Yule-log, that

blazes so bright;

Round which cottars sit, on a

cold Christmas night.

Yew, a long-lived, and dark shadowy tree,

That often in old country churchyards we see.

Yacht, a small vessel, so nice for a sail;

That skims like a bird, in a favouring gale.

Gay Yellow-hammer, a sweet lively bird.

York, of whose Minster most people have heard.

Yoke, that connects those two oxen, so strong,

The lad in the picture is leading along.

Yeoman, an officer, well known at court.

Yarmouth, a place to which bathers resort.

Yarrow, a weed that we find in the fields.

Yam, a nice root that America yields.

Yawl, a ship's boat, that we saw on the shore,

The day that papa took us all to the Nore.

" Yes," the dear word mamma said, as she smiled,

When I asked, with a kiss, if she loved her fond child?

Youth, life's short morning, that soon will be o'er:

Oh waste not the hours that will come back no more.

the last letter, but

seldom we need,

As you will discover, when books

you can read.

Z begins **Z**enith, the sky overhead,

Where shines the pale moon, as we lie in our bed.

Also **Z**accheus, who climbed up a tree,

That, as he was short, he the Saviour might see.

Zephyr, the breeze, so refreshing and cool.

Zebra, a pretty striped species of mule.

Zechin, a coin that at Venice they use.

King **Z**edekiah, who reigned o'er the Jews.

Also **Z**oological Gardens, where Ned

One day went to see the wild animals fed.

Zion, the hill where the Temple, of old,

Stood fair in the sunlight, all marble and gold.

Zenas, a lawyer—disciple of Paul:

Ziba, too, one of the servants of Saul.

Zarephath, where dwelt the widow's sick son.

Zebedee, father of James and of John.

Zealous, like Alfred, who still strives to excel:

Without **Z**eal, we scarce can do anything well.

And now, dear child, that you have read
The alphabet, from A to Z,
You've found each letter, in its turn,
Suggest you something good to learn;
Something that you, another day,
May think of, in your work or play,

These letters, when combined in rows,
The largest, longest book compose:
Look, therefore, at each letter well,
And soon you'll learn to read and spell;
And oh, how pleased I then shall be,
To hear you read nice books to me!

And oh, how much more pleased, my dear,
While you in learning persevere,
To see you in your youth begin
To honour God, and flee from sin;
To watch you day by day progress
In wisdom, virtue, holiness.

Oh early to the Saviour come;
Still at His loving feet there's room.
Seek, little lamb, the Shepherd's care:
Go with this simple lisping prayer—
" Lord, cleanse this sinful heart of mine;
And make me wholly, wholly, thine."

S. W. P.